NOVE

SAINT

STEPHEN

Unfailing 9 Days Powerful and Sacred
Prayer to Saint Stephen Patron Saint of
Deacons, Alter Servers, Casket Makers

CHARLOTTE SMITH

Copyright © Charlotte Smith, 2023

Introduction

Saint Stephen, who passed away in 36 CE in Jerusalem, is revered as the first Christian martyr. His defense before the Sanhedrin, as recorded in Acts of the Apostles 7, reveals a distinctive belief within early Christianity. Stephen's unwavering faith, presented before the rabbinic court, stirred anger among the Jewish audience, leading to his tragic stoning outside the city. His final words, echoing Jesus on the cross (Luke 23:34), were a prayer of forgiveness for his attackers.

Recognized as the patron saint of deacons and stonemasons, Saint Stephen is commemorated on December 26. The name Stephen, of Greek origin, is attributed to a

Hellenist—a foreign-born Jew fluent in Greek. Living in Jerusalem, he embraced Christianity.

In Acts of the Apostles 6, it is revealed that Stephen was among the seven deacons appointed to address concerns, notably the care of elderly widows, raised by Hellenist converts within the early Christian community. His evangelistic gifts and engagement in religious discussions marked him as a prominent figure.

Stephen's speech before the Sanhedrin reflected both Jewish concerns and Hellenistic rhetorical conventions. Scholars propose a potential Samaritan connection to Stephen's community, suggesting a migration after the destruction of Jerusalem in 70 CE. Stephen's opposition to the Temple cult and sacrificial practices, coupled with his reverence for the Law of Moses, defined his theological stance. He considered the Temple's construction akin to idolatry and emphasized the divine dwelling beyond man-made structures.

While the Temple held significance for many early Christians, Stephen's viewpoint was uniquely critical. Unlike others, he did not assign doctrinal significance to Jesus' death, yet he may have been among the first to anticipate the Second Coming. In a moment of spiritual revelation, he envisioned "the Son of Man standing at the right hand of God," using a term predominantly employed by Jesus himself.

Stephen's faith seemed rooted in both old and new traditions, representing a pre-Pauline Christian movement that has become challenging to decipher due to subsequent transformations.

Background

Saint Stephen, recognized as the inaugural Christian martyr, is thought to have been born approximately in the year 5 AD, though the precise date remains elusive. His birthplace was Jerusalem, and he belonged to a devout Jewish family. While historical records lack specific details about his family members, it is acknowledged that he spent his formative years within a Jewish community.

First introduced in the Acts of the Apostles, Stephen emerged as one of seven deacons chosen by the Apostles. Their primary role was to administer food and charitable assistance to the less fortunate members of the early church community. Orthodox tradition designates him as the "archdeacon," believed to be the eldest among the deacons. Although another deacon, Nicholas of Antioch, is noted as a convert to Judaism, Stephen's Jewish background is implied, with limited information about his earlier life. The appointment of deacons aimed to address dissatisfaction among Hellenistic Jews, particularly those influenced by Greek culture and language, who felt their widows were overlooked in favor of Hebraic widows in the daily distribution of provisions.

The name "Stephanos" being of Greek origin has led to the assumption that Stephen was one of these Hellenistic Jews. Acts of the Apostles describes him as replete with faith and the Holy Spirit, performing miracles among the people.

Stephen's teachings and miracles appear to have taken place within synagogues of Hellenistic Jews, as evidenced by the opposition he faced from the "Synagogue of the Freedmen," as well as groups from Cyrene, Alexandria, Cilicia, and Asia. Despite challenges to his teachings, Stephen prevailed in debates, leading to the adversaries fabricating false accusations of blasphemy against Moses and God. Subsequently, he was brought before the Sanhedrin, the highest Jewish legal court, accused of speaking against the Temple and the Mosaic Law. Remarkably unperturbed, Stephen's countenance was described as resembling "that of an angel."

Speech to Sanhedrin

In an extensive address to the Sanhedrin, spanning nearly the entirety of Acts chapter 7, Stephen shares his perspective on the history of Israel. He begins by emphasizing that the God of glory appeared to Abraham in Mesopotamia, a key theme throughout his speech, asserting that God's presence transcends any specific structure, such as the Temple. Stephen delves into the narratives of the patriarchs, providing detailed accounts, with a particular focus on Moses. He highlights how God revealed Himself to Moses through the burning bush, inspiring him to lead the Israelites out of Egypt. Despite these divine interventions, the Israelites deviated to worship other gods, illustrating the second central theme of

Stephen's speech—Israel's disobedience to God.

Stephen faced two specific accusations: firstly, that he predicted Jesus would destroy the Temple in Jerusalem, and secondly, that he altered the established customs of Moses. In 2012, Pope Benedict XVI noted that St. Stephen utilized Jewish scriptures to demonstrate that Jesus did not undermine the laws of Moses but rather fulfilled them. Stephen confronts his audience, labeling them as "stiff-necked" individuals who, like their forebearers, resist the Holy Spirit. He accuses them of a historical pattern of persecuting prophets, even going so far as to kill those who foretold the arrival of the Righteous One. Stephen boldly concludes, accusing his listeners of betraying and murdering the prophesied Messiah.

The stoning of Stephen

Following the severe rebuke, the narrative unfolds with the crowd unable to contain their anger. In this heated moment, Stephen, undeterred, looked up and exclaimed, "Look! I see heaven open and the Son of Man standing on the right hand of God!" He conveyed that Jesus, recently resurrected, stood beside God. The infuriated crowd, instigated to violence, cast the first stones and placed their coats at the feet of a "young man named Saul," later revealed as Paul the Apostle.

Even in the face of impending harm, Stephen uttered a prayer, asking the Lord to receive his spirit and extending forgiveness to his killers. He then knelt, and, in a poignant phrase, "fell asleep." Meanwhile, Saul not only witnessed but also approved of Stephen's execution. Following Stephen's tragic demise, the remaining disciples, with the exception of the apostles, dispersed to distant lands, many finding refuge in Antioch.

Location of the martyrdom

The account of Stephen's stoning in Acts doesn't specify the exact site, leading to two distinct traditions. According to renowned French archaeologists Louis-Hugues Vincent (1872–1960) and Félix-Marie Abel (1878–1953), one tradition, believed to be ancient, posits the event occurred at Jerusalem's northern gate. Conversely, another tradition, dated by Vincent and Abel to the Middle Ages and no earlier than the 12th century, places the stoning at the eastern gate.

The ambiguity in the historical record has given rise to these differing perspectives on the location of this significant event.

Views of Stephen's speech

Among the various speeches found in Acts of the Apostles, Stephen's address to the Sanhedrin stands out as the lengthiest. Some skepticism has been raised about the accuracy of reproducing such an extensive speech in the text of Acts exactly as it was originally delivered. In response to this concern, certain Biblical scholars propose that the speech reveals a distinctive personality behind it.

There are at least five instances where Stephen's recounting of Israelite history diverges from the scriptures where these stories originated. For example, Stephen mentions Jacob's tomb being in Shechem, whereas Genesis 50:13 indicates that Jacob's body was carried and buried in a cave in Machpelah at Hebron. Some theologians argue that these divergences may not be discrepancies but rather a condensation of historical events for an audience already familiar with them. While not recorded in Genesis, the possibility that Jacob's bones were transferred to Shechem for a final burial, as with Joseph's bones according to Joshua 24:32, is considered. However, other scholars view them as errors, and some interpret them as deliberate choices conveying theological points. Alternatively, these differences could stem from an ancient Jewish tradition not included in the scriptures or prevalent among non-scribe residents of Jerusalem.

Noteworthy parallels between Stephen's accounts in Acts and the life of Jesus in the Gospels, including performing miracles, facing Sanhedrin trials, and praying for forgiveness for their killers, have led to suspicions that the author of Acts may have emphasized or even invented some or all of these elements to illustrate that people become holy when following Christ's example.

Stephen's speech is marked by strong criticism of traditional Jewish belief and practice. For instance, his assertion that God does not reside in a dwelling "made by human hands," referring to the Temple, echoes language often used in Biblical texts to describe idols. Some critics, including the priest and scholar S. G. F. Brandon, have labeled the speech as anti-Judaic, suggesting that it reflects the author of Acts' attitude toward Judaism.

Tomb and relics of Stephen

According to Acts 8:2, it's mentioned that "Godly men buried Stephen and mourned deeply for him," yet the specific location of his burial is not specified.

In the year 415, a priest named Lucian reportedly had a dream revealing the location of Stephen's remains at Beit Jimal. Subsequently, the relics of the protomartyr were solemnly processed to the Church of Hagia Sion on December 26, 415, establishing this date as the feast of Saint Stephen. Avitus of Braga, involved in a plan to bring some relics to Braga, documented the recovery of these relics in a letter. In

439, the relics were transferred to a new church constructed by Empress Aelia Eudocia north of the Damascus Gate in honor of Saint Stephen. This church, unfortunately, was destroyed in the 12th century. In its place, a 20th-century French Catholic church named Saint-Étienne was erected, alongside the Greek Orthodox Church of St Stephen, which was built outside the eastern gate of the city. There are two traditions regarding the site of Stephen's martyrdom—one placing it at the northern location outside Damascus Gate and the other at the eastern gate.

During the Crusader period, the main northern gate of Jerusalem was called "Saint Stephen's Gate" due to its proximity to the church and monastery built by Empress

Eudocia. However, after the disappearance of the Byzantine church, the name was transferred to the accessible eastern gate. This name persists to this day.

The relics of the protomartyr were later translated to Rome by Pope Pelagius II during the construction of the basilica of San Lorenzo fuori le Mura. They were interred alongside the relics of Saint Lawrence, and according to the Golden Legend, the relics of Lawrence miraculously made room for those of Stephen.

The Imperial Regalia of the Holy Roman Empire includes a relic known as St. Stephen's Purse, an ornate box believed to contain soil soaked with the blood of St. Stephen, likely created in the 9th century.

In Augustine of Hippo's book, The City of God, he describes numerous miracles associated with the relics of Saint Stephen when part of them was brought to Africa.

Saint Stephen's Day

Western Christianity

In Western Christianity, December 26 is designated as "Saint Stephen's Day" or the "Feast of Stephen," a term familiarized by the English Christmas carol "Good King Wenceslas." This day holds the status of a public holiday in numerous nations with historical Catholic, Anglican, and Lutheran traditions. Among these countries are Austria, Croatia, the Czech Republic, Hungary, Ireland, Luxembourg, Slovakia, Poland, Italy, Germany, Norway, Sweden, Denmark, Finland, Catalonia, and the Balearic Isles. Interestingly, in Australia, New Zealand, Canada, and the United Kingdom, December 26 is celebrated as "Boxing Day."

Within the contemporary liturgy of the Roman Catholic Church, the feast is commemorated during the Eucharist. However, for the Liturgy of the Hours, the celebration is confined to the daytime hours, with Evening Prayer reserved for the celebration of the Octave of Christmas. Historically, the "Invention of the Relics of Saint Stephen," marking the purported discovery of his relics, was observed on August 3. Both the feasts of December 26 and August 3 have been referenced in dating clauses within historical documents originating from England. The Church of England commemorates Stephen with a Festival on December 26.

Eastern Christianity

In the Eastern Orthodox Church, Eastern Catholic Churches following the Byzantine Rite, and Oriental Orthodox Churches such as Coptic, Syrian, and Malankara, Saint Stephen's feast day is celebrated on December 27. This timing is a result of the Synaxis of the Theotokos being observed on December 26. Consequently, this arrangement also shifts the Feast of the Holy Innocents to December 29. The day is often referred to as the "Third Day of the Nativity" because it marks the third day of the Christmas season.

Certain Orthodox churches, particularly those in the west, adhere to a modified Julian calendar aligning date names with the widely used Gregorian calendar. In these churches, the observed date for the feast is recognized as December 27. However, other Orthodox churches, including the Oriental Orthodox, maintain the original Julian calendar. Throughout the 21st century, December 27 Julian will consistently correspond to January 9 in the Gregorian calendar, and this is the date on which they observe the feast.

9 DAYS NOVENA PRAYER TO SAINT STEPHEN, PATRON SAINT OF DEACONS, ALTER SERVERS AND CASKET MAKERS.

(Begin with the sign of the Cross, Precede with an opening Prayer, Say the Prayer and silently ask your personal intentions. Conclude each day by reciting one Our Father... one Hail Mary... one Glory Be...)

Day 1

Let us commence. In the name of the Father, and of the Son, and of the Holy Spirit. Amen.

O illustrious St. Stephen, the first Martyr for the Faith, overflowing with empathy for those who call upon you and with love for those enduring hardship, burdened as I am with the weight of my troubles. I humbly kneel before you, entreating you to extend your special protection to my current necessity...

(mention your request here…)

Kindly recommend it to our Lord Jesus, and persist in your intercession until my plea

finds favor. Above all, obtain for me the grace to eventually behold God face to face, joining you, Mary, and all the heavenly beings in eternal praise. Mighty Saint Stephen, Deacon and martyr, shield me from losing my soul and secure for me the grace to attain everlasting joy in heaven.

Saint Stephen, intercede for us.

Say 1: Our Father... Say 1: Hail Mary... Say 1: Glory Be...

REFLECTIONS

"Now Stephen, a man full of God's grace and power, performed great wonders and signs among the people." (Acts 6:8)

Day 2

Let us commence. In the name of the Father, and of the Son, and of the Holy Spirit. Amen.

O illustrious St. Stephen, the first Martyr for the Faith, overflowing with empathy for those who call upon you and with love for those enduring hardship, burdened as I am with the weight of my troubles. I humbly kneel before you, entreating you to extend your special protection to my current necessity...

(mention your request here…)

Kindly recommend it to our Lord Jesus, and persist in your intercession until my plea

finds favor. Above all, obtain for me the grace to eventually behold God face to face, joining you, Mary, and all the heavenly beings in eternal praise. Mighty Saint Stephen, Deacon and martyr, shield me from losing my soul and secure for me the grace to attain everlasting joy in heaven.

Saint Stephen, intercede for us.

Say 1: Our Father... Say 1: Hail Mary... Say 1: Glory Be...

REFLECTIONS

"When the members of the Sanhedrin heard this, they were furious and gnashed their teeth at him... While they were stoning him, Stephen prayed, 'Lord Jesus, receive my spirit.'" (Acts 7:54-60)

Day 3

Let us commence. In the name of the Father, and of the Son, and of the Holy Spirit. Amen.

O illustrious St. Stephen, the first Martyr for the Faith, overflowing with empathy for those who call upon you and with love for those enduring hardship, burdened as I am with the weight of my troubles. I humbly kneel before you, entreating you to extend your special protection to my current necessity...

(mention your request here…)

Kindly recommend it to our Lord Jesus, and persist in your intercession until my plea

finds favor. Above all, obtain for me the grace to eventually behold God face to face, joining you, Mary, and all the heavenly beings in eternal praise. Mighty Saint Stephen, Deacon and martyr, shield me from losing my soul and secure for me the grace to attain everlasting joy in heaven.

Saint Stephen, intercede for us.

Say 1: Our Father… Say 1: Hail Mary… Say 1: Glory Be…

REFLECTIONS

"On my account you will be brought before governors and kings as witnesses to them and to the Gentiles." (Matthew 10:18)

Day 4

Let us commence. In the name of the Father, and of the Son, and of the Holy Spirit. Amen.

O illustrious St. Stephen, the first Martyr for the Faith, overflowing with empathy for those who call upon you and with love for those enduring hardship, burdened as I am with the weight of my troubles. I humbly kneel before you, entreating you to extend your special protection to my current necessity...

(mention your request here…)

Kindly recommend it to our Lord Jesus, and persist in your intercession until my plea

finds favor. Above all, obtain for me the grace to eventually behold God face to face, joining you, Mary, and all the heavenly beings in eternal praise. Mighty Saint Stephen, Deacon and martyr, shield me from losing my soul and secure for me the grace to attain everlasting joy in heaven.

Saint Stephen, intercede for us.

Say 1: Our Father... Say 1: Hail Mary... Say 1: Glory Be...

REFLECTIONS

"Blessed are those who are persecuted because of righteousness, for theirs is the kingdom of heaven." (Matthew 5:10)

Day 5

Let us commence. In the name of the Father, and of the Son, and of the Holy Spirit. Amen.

O illustrious St. Stephen, the first Martyr for the Faith, overflowing with empathy for those who call upon you and with love for those enduring hardship, burdened as I am with the weight of my troubles. I humbly kneel before you, entreating you to extend your special protection to my current necessity...

(mention your request here...)

Kindly recommend it to our Lord Jesus, and persist in your intercession until my plea

finds favor. Above all, obtain for me the grace to eventually behold God face to face, joining you, Mary, and all the heavenly beings in eternal praise. Mighty Saint Stephen, Deacon and martyr, shield me from losing my soul and secure for me the grace to attain everlasting joy in heaven.

Saint Stephen, intercede for us.

Say 1: Our Father... Say 1: Hail Mary... Say 1: Glory Be...

REFLECTIONS

"In fact, everyone who wants to live a godly life in Christ Jesus will be persecuted." (2 Timothy 3:12)

Day 6

Let us commence. In the name of the Father, and of the Son, and of the Holy Spirit. Amen.

O illustrious St. Stephen, the first Martyr for the Faith, overflowing with empathy for those who call upon you and with love for those enduring hardship, burdened as I am with the weight of my troubles. I humbly kneel before you, entreating you to extend your special protection to my current necessity...

(mention your request here...)

Kindly recommend it to our Lord Jesus, and persist in your intercession until my plea

finds favor. Above all, obtain for me the grace to eventually behold God face to face, joining you, Mary, and all the heavenly beings in eternal praise. Mighty Saint Stephen, Deacon and martyr, shield me from losing my soul and secure for me the grace to attain everlasting joy in heaven.

Saint Stephen, intercede for us.

Say 1: Our Father... Say 1: Hail Mary... Say 1: Glory Be...

REFLECTIONS

"But make up your mind not to worry beforehand how you will defend yourselves. For I will give you words and wisdom that none of your adversaries will be able to resist or contradict." (Luke 21:14-15)

Day 7

Let us commence. In the name of the Father, and of the Son, and of the Holy Spirit. Amen.

O illustrious St. Stephen, the first Martyr for the Faith, overflowing with empathy for those who call upon you and with love for those enduring hardship, burdened as I am with the weight of my troubles. I humbly kneel before you, entreating you to extend your special protection to my current necessity...

(mention your request here…)

Kindly recommend it to our Lord Jesus, and persist in your intercession until my plea

finds favor. Above all, obtain for me the grace to eventually behold God face to face, joining you, Mary, and all the heavenly beings in eternal praise. Mighty Saint Stephen, Deacon and martyr, shield me from losing my soul and secure for me the grace to attain everlasting joy in heaven.

Saint Stephen, intercede for us.

Say 1: Our Father... Say 1: Hail Mary... Say 1: Glory Be...

REFLECTIONS

"But even if you should suffer for what is right, you are blessed. 'Do not fear their threats; do not be frightened.'" (1 Peter 3:14)

Day 8

Let us commence. In the name of the Father, and of the Son, and of the Holy Spirit. Amen.

O illustrious St. Stephen, the first Martyr for the Faith, overflowing with empathy for those who call upon you and with love for those enduring hardship, burdened as I am with the weight of my troubles. I humbly kneel before you, entreating you to extend your special protection to my current necessity...

(mention your request here…)

Kindly recommend it to our Lord Jesus, and persist in your intercession until my plea

finds favor. Above all, obtain for me the grace to eventually behold God face to face, joining you, Mary, and all the heavenly beings in eternal praise. Mighty Saint Stephen, Deacon and martyr, shield me from losing my soul and secure for me the grace to attain everlasting joy in heaven.

Saint Stephen, intercede for us.

Say 1: Our Father... Say 1: Hail Mary... Say 1: Glory Be...

REFLECTIONS

"If the world hates you, keep in mind that it hated me first. If you belonged to the world, it would love you as its own." (John 15:18-19)

Day 9

Let us commence. In the name of the Father, and of the Son, and of the Holy Spirit. Amen.

O illustrious St. Stephen, the first Martyr for the Faith, overflowing with empathy for those who call upon you and with love for those enduring hardship, burdened as I am with the weight of my troubles. I humbly kneel before you, entreating you to extend your special protection to my current necessity...

(mention your request here…)

Kindly recommend it to our Lord Jesus, and persist in your intercession until my plea

finds favor. Above all, obtain for me the grace to eventually behold God face to face, joining you, Mary, and all the heavenly beings in eternal praise. Mighty Saint Stephen, Deacon and martyr, shield me from losing my soul and secure for me the grace to attain everlasting joy in heaven.

Saint Stephen, intercede for us.

Say 1: Our Father... Say 1: Hail Mary... Say 1: Glory Be...

REFLECTIONS

"I consider that our present sufferings are not worth comparing with the glory that will be revealed in us." (Romans 8:18)

Printed in Great Britain
by Amazon